50 Great Kitchens by Architects

50 Great Kitchens by Architects

Edited by Aisha Hasanovic

images
Publishing

First published in Australia in 2005 by
The Images Publishing Group Pty Ltd
ABN 89 059 734 431
6 Bastow Place, Mulgrave, Victoria, 3170, Australia
Telephone: +61 3 9561 5544 Facsimile: +61 3 9561 4860
books@images.com.au
www.imagespublishing.com

National Library of Australia
Cataloguing-in-Publication data

50 great kitchens by architects.

Includes index.

ISBN 1 92074 470 3.

1. Kitchens—Pictorial works. 2. Kitchens—Design and construction.
747.797

Co-ordinating editor: Aisha Hasanovic

Designed by The Graphic Image Studio Pty Ltd, Mulgrave, 3170, Australia
www.tgis.com.au

Film by SC (Sang Choy) International Pte Ltd
Printed by Everbest Printing Co. Ltd, in Hong Kong/China

A kitchen's relation to its surrounding rooms, the play of light, the positioning of the equipment and appliances, as well as additional features, are important. Should the cabinets and benches line the walls, or should a large island be the central focus? What materials can be used other than wood for cabinets, tiles for floors and marble for bench tops? Whether a kitchen is being renovated or designed as part of a new home, the role of the architect is invaluable. A kitchen needs to be functional as well as aesthetically pleasing.

50 Great Kitchens by Architects is primarily an ideas book, highlighting a diverse range of architecturally designed kitchens through full-color photographs, plans, and simple captions. We have selected projects by many of the world's most talented architects that show an innovative use of materials, and traditional as well as modern color schemes for the reader seeking ideas for a new kitchen, or planning a major renovation.

The importance of the architect in determining a kitchen's design is emphasized, and each individual kitchen is accompanied by a personal comment from the architect: whether it is a description of their favorite feature or what they feel to be the most important element of their kitchen design.

Whenever possible, floor plans indicate the position of the kitchen within the building, or a simplified plan shows a basic layout. The kitchens are shaded on the plans to make them distinguishable. Approximate scales in feet and meters, together with north arrows give further insight into the size and location of many of the featured kitchens.

Aisha Hasanovic
Editor

"The double-height space brings light into the kitchen from all directions" MCINTURFF ARCHITECTS

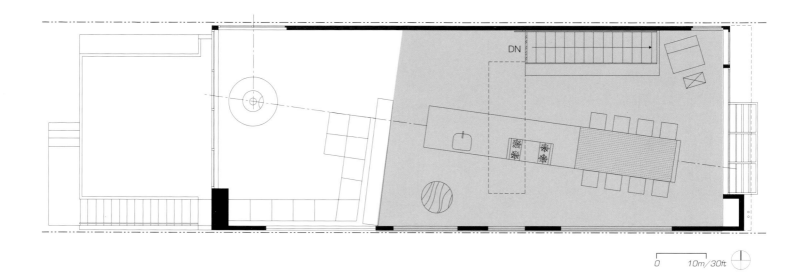

"Stainless steel assemblage extends to become the walnut dining table" CCS ARCHITECTURE

10

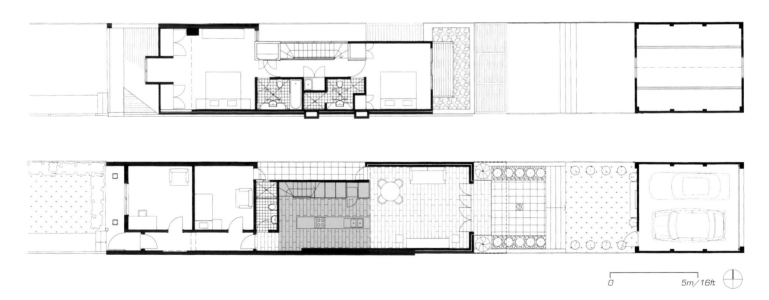

0   5m/16ft

"Servery and suspended range hood form sculptural elements" CULLEN FENG

"Large sliding panel screens kitchen from living and dining area" STANIC HARDING

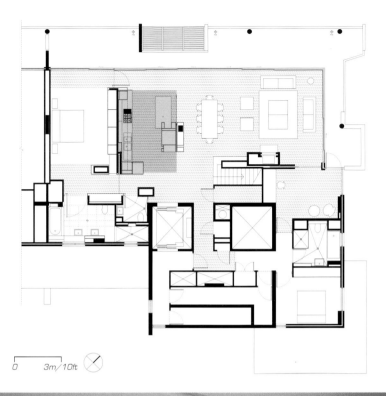

0   3m/10ft

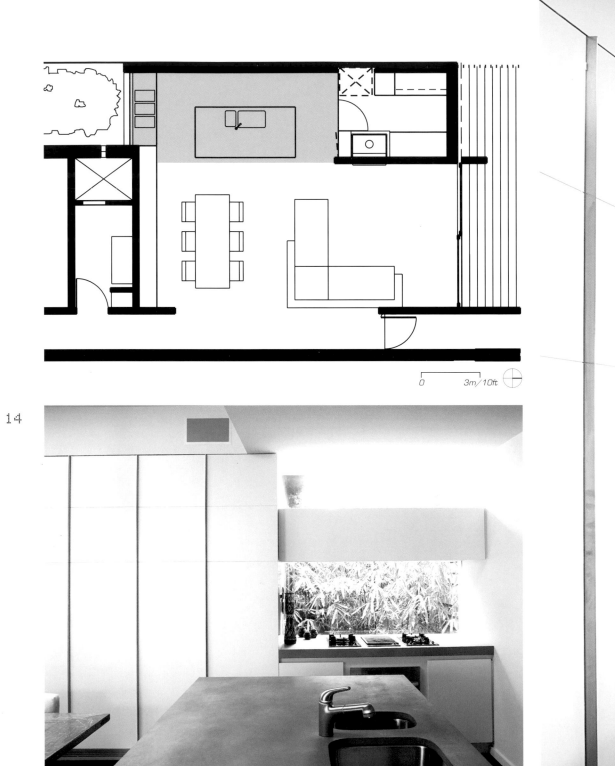

14

"Work bench is large" STEPHEN JOLSON ARCHITECT PTY LTD

0   3m/10ft

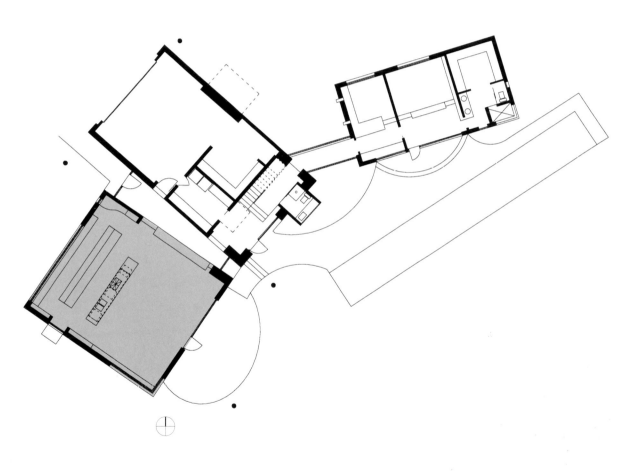

17

"A native mesquite wood counter complements the birch cabinets" IBARRA ROSANO DESIGN ARCHITECTS

"Continuous use of stainless steel on curved wall, fixtures, and appliances" GRAFT

"Wooden sliding wall opens the kitchen to the living areas" OFIS ARHITEKTI

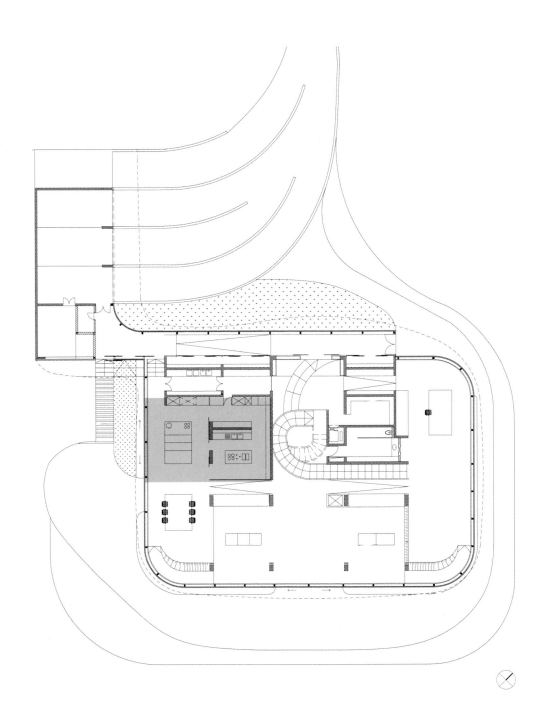

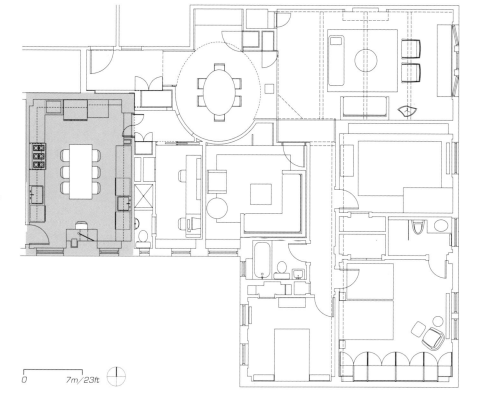

26

0   7m/23ft

"Cabinets line the perimeter, maximizing the kitchen space" RESOLUTION: 4 ARCHITECTURE

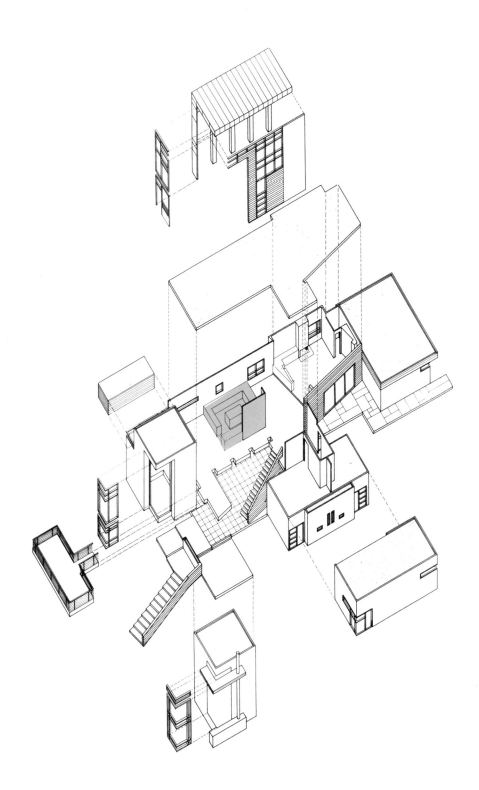

28

"There are views in every direction" STUDIO 9ONE2 ARCHITECTURE

"Opening to patio establishes connections to landscape" CCS ARCHITECTURE

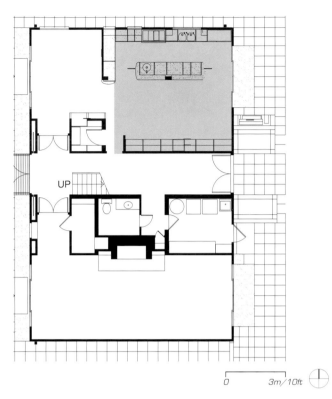

UP

0   3m/10ft

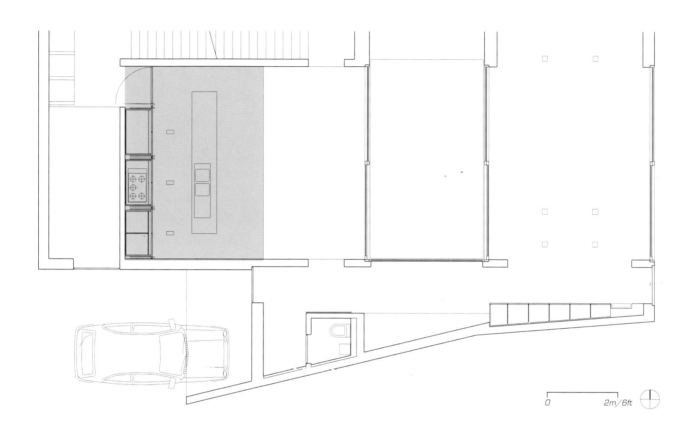

0   2m/6ft

"Shelving and cooking are concealed behind sliding doors" ARCHITECTENLAB

36

"Style is casual and cottage-like" GOOD ARCHITECTURE

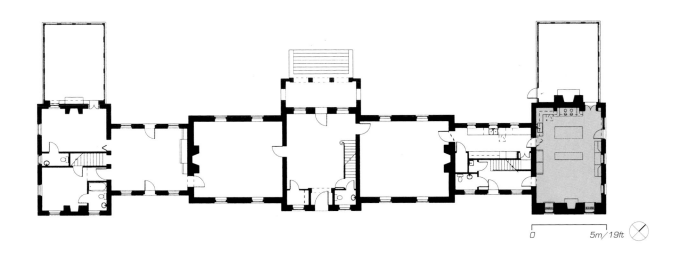

0   5m/19ft

0   2m/6ft

"Counter and overhead cupboards frame the view to the garden" CONNOR + SOLOMON ARCHITECTS

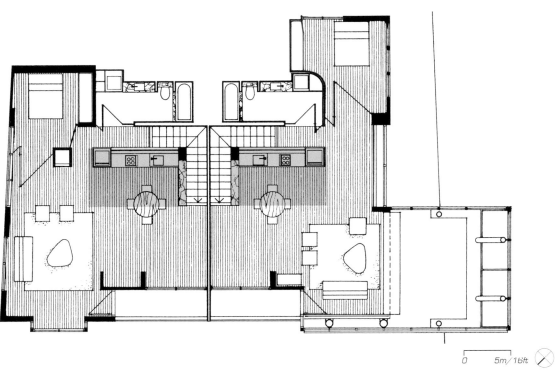

"Translucent splashback brings light to stairwell behind" STANIC HARDING

"Island and dining table appear stage-like against the backdrop of cabinets" RESOLUTION:4 ARCHITECTURE

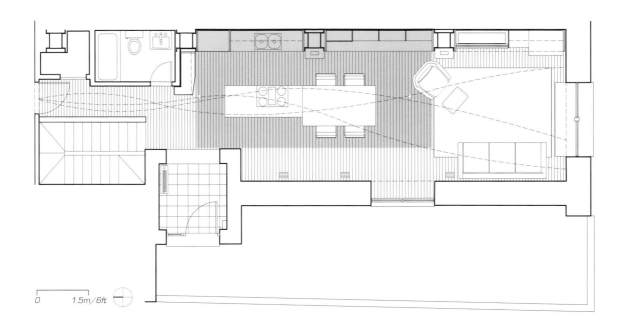

0   1.5m/6ft

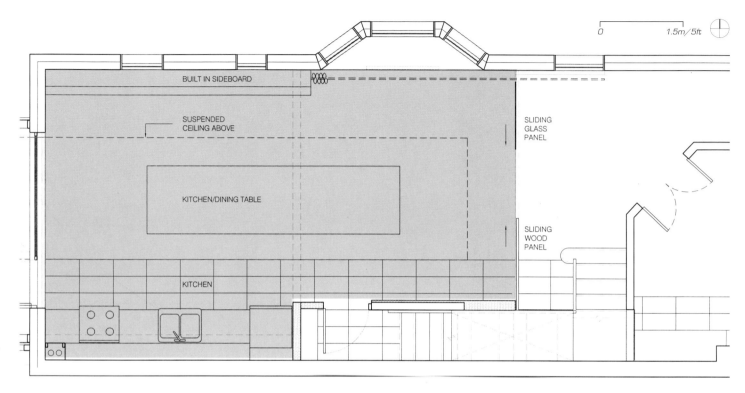

BUILT IN SIDEBOARD

SUSPENDED
CEILING ABOVE

SLIDING
GLASS
PANEL

KITCHEN/DINING TABLE

SLIDING
WOOD
PANEL

KITCHEN

0   1.5m / 5ft

"Caters for everyday family living as well as great entertaining" 3RD UNCLE DESIGN

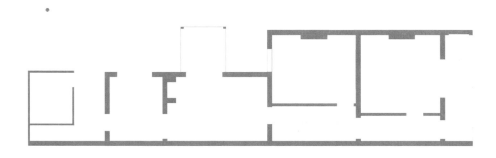

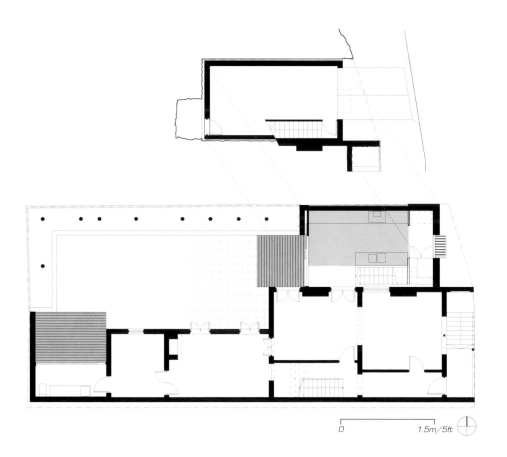

0　　　　　　　　　1.5m/5ft

"Massive concrete bench structures shape the interior language" CONNOR + SOLOMON ARCHITECTS

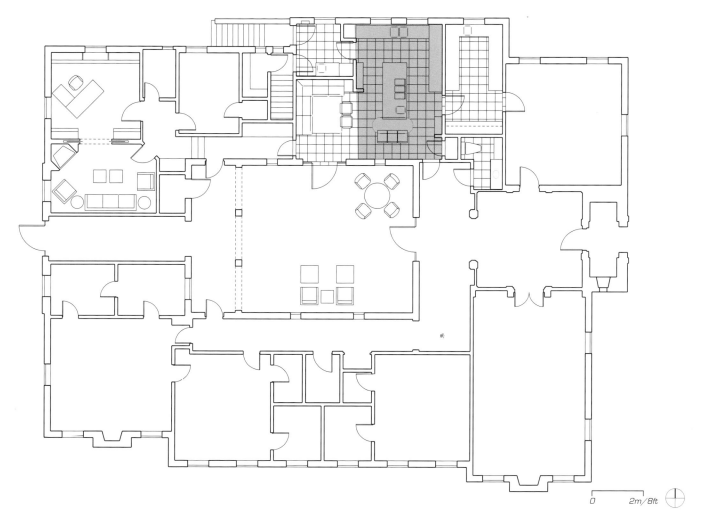

49

0   2m/8ft

"The kitchen is not defined by walls" STEPHEN JOLSON ARCHITECT PTY LTD

"Kitchen table adds flexibility to the space" SUPERKÜL INC ARCHITECT

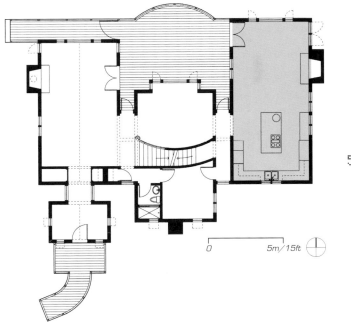

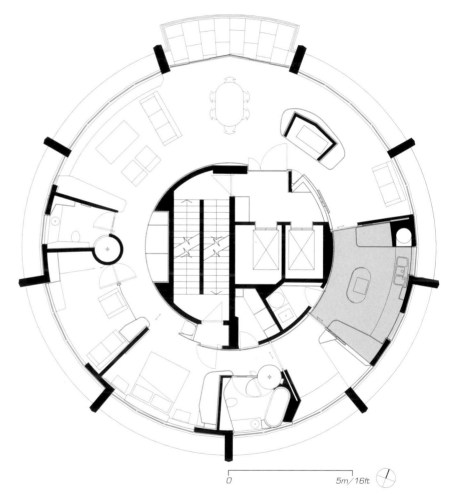

0   5m/16ft

"Central curved island unit contains storage below and range hood above" STANIC HARDING

"180-year-old spotted-gum timber benches look like stacked blocks" STEPHEN JOLSON ARCHITECT PTY LTD

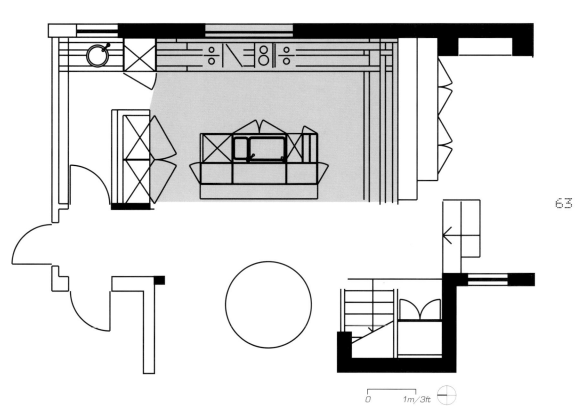

0   1m/3ft

"Off-the-shelf materials like plywood and plastic laminate have been used creatively" ARCHIMANIA

"The good-sized kitchen island is great for parties" SUPERKÜL INC ARCHITECT

"Volumetric play between cherry cabinetry and stainless steel appliances" CHA & INNERHOFER ARCHITECTURE + DESIGN

"Mirrors lining the walls visually enlarge the compact space" DAVID HICKS PTY LTD

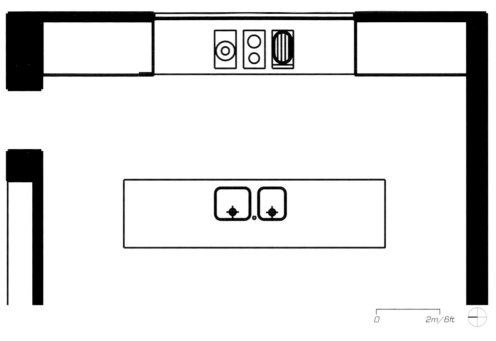

"Glass splashback offers view into uplit bamboo garden" STEPHEN JOLSON ARCHITECT PTY LTD

"Jarrah, veneer, and granite contrast warmly with black glass tiles" IREDALE PEDERSEN HOOK ARCHITECTS

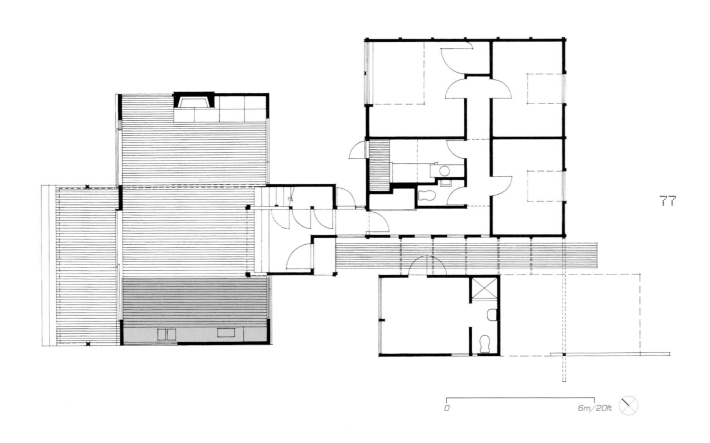

"The bench continues the lines of the architecture" PARSONSON ARCHITECTS

0 ⊢————————⊣ 6m/20ft

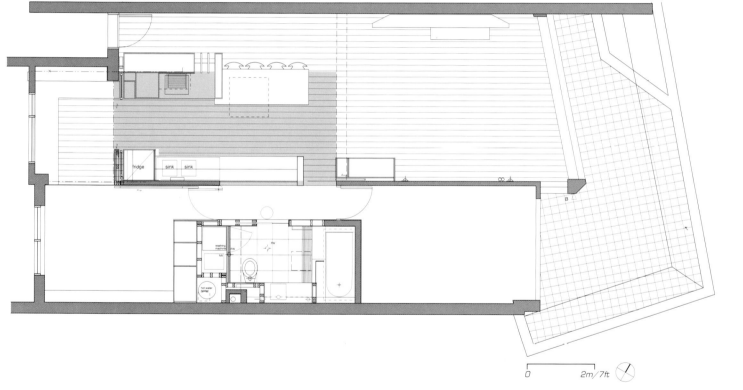

fridge | sink | sink

washing machine | tub

hot water heater

B

0   2m/7ft

"Kitchen frames view" STANIC HARDING

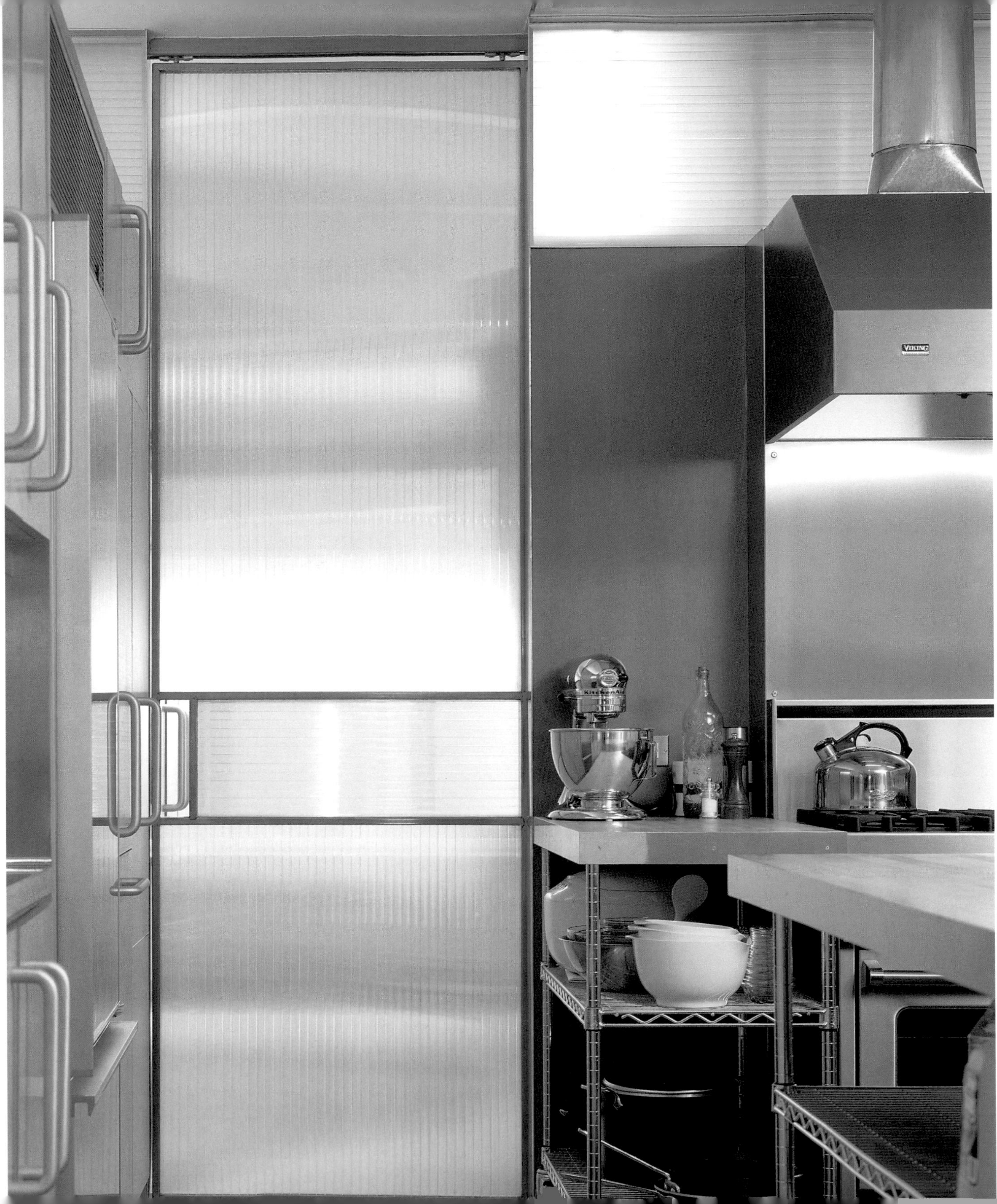
VIKING
KitchenAid

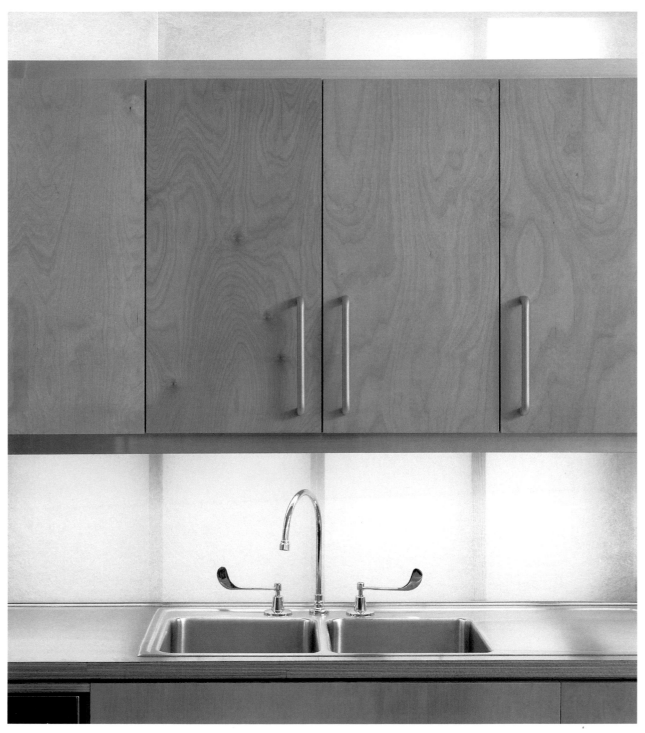

"Simple materials have been arranged to create a modern custom kitchen" RESOLUTION:4 ARCHITECTURE

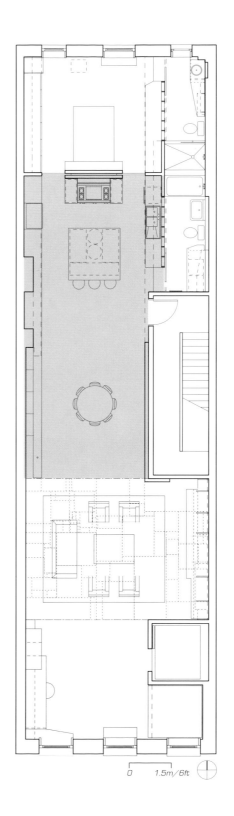

0   1.5m/6ft

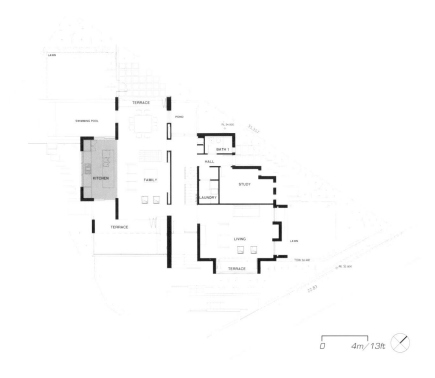

LAWN

TERRACE

SWIMMING POOL

POND

RL 34.300

35.352

BATH 1

HALL

KITCHEN

FAMILY

STUDY

LAUNDRY

TERRACE

LIVING

LAWN

TOW 34.440

RE 32.800

TERRACE

22.83

0   4m/13ft

"Kitchen enjoys views to harbor" CORBEN

"Joinery forms a picture-frame around cooking activity zone" INTERLANDI MANTESSO ARCHITECTS

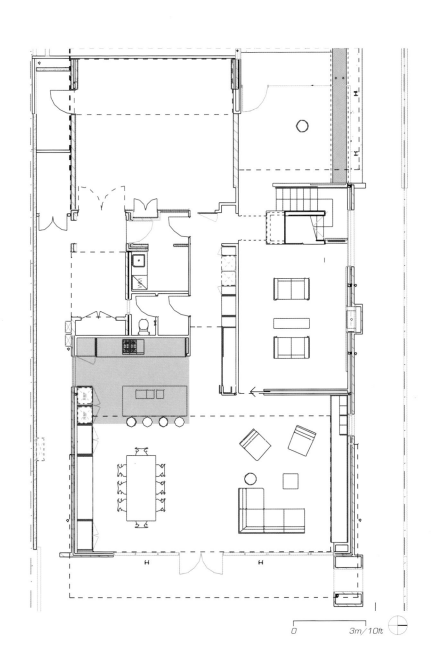

0   3m / 10ft

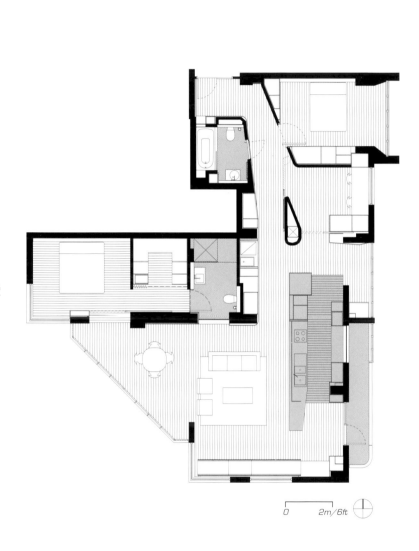

0   2m/6ft

"The kitchen is a sculptural element within the apartment" STANIC HARDING

"Central kitchen is accessible to outdoors and owners' art collection"
SHUBIN + DONALDSON ARCHITECTS

"Island bench is multifunctional and storage is concealed" POD INTERIOR DESIGN

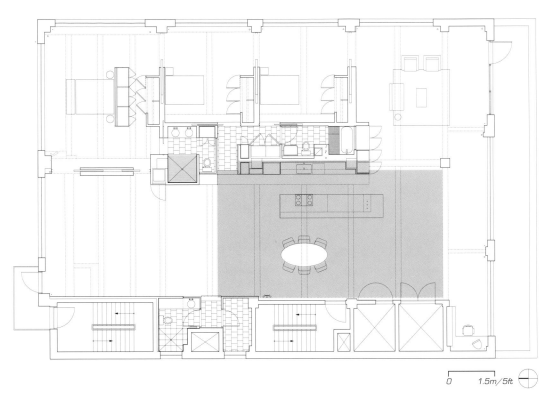

0   1.5m/5ft

"Teak island doubles as a piece of furniture" RESOLUTION:4 ARCHITECTURE

"The earthy tones meld modern and Mexican elements" SHUBIN + DONALDSON ARCHITECTS

102

"The space is neat and compact" RESOLUTION:4 ARCHITECTURE

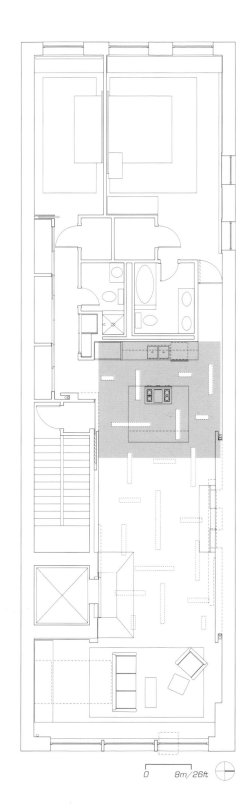

105

"The ceiling has a downward flow" DALE JONES-EVANS PTY LTD ARCHITECTURE

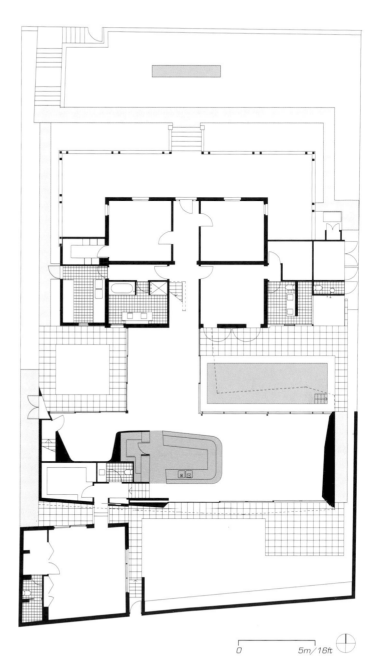

0   5m / 16ft

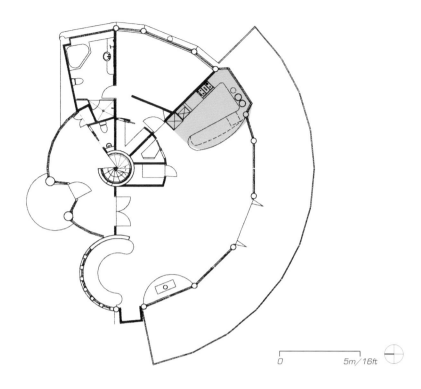

0 ———— 5m/16ft

"Embracing sensational views" MURRAY COCKBURN PARTNERSHIP

"Use of white complements natural timbers and stone" BRENT HULENA

113

"1950's diner area adds enhancement" MARK CUTLER DESIGN

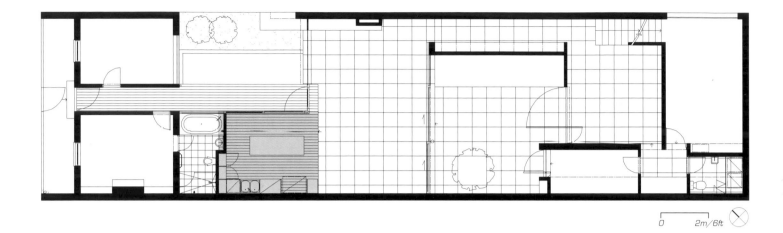

"External walls slide away extending the kitchen into the courtyard" COY & YIONTIS

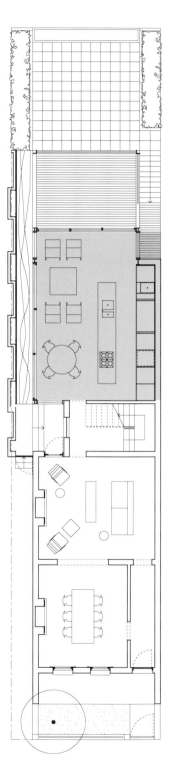

0   2m/6ft

"Kitchen extends beyond the glass line into an outdoor room" ENGELEN MOORE

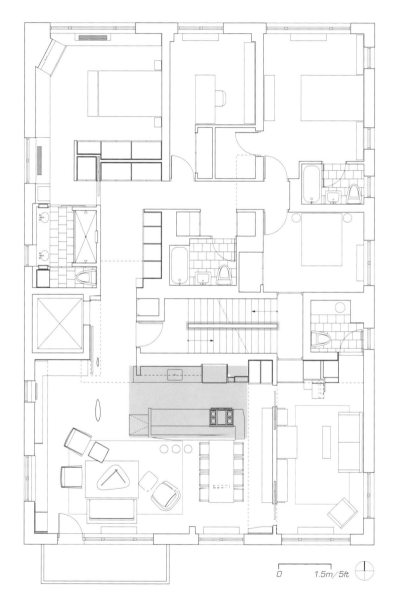

"Integrated dining table and kitchen island demarcate zones of use" RESOLUTION:4 ARCHITECTURE

"Generous space allows for informal entertaining while cooking" CCS ARCHITECTURE

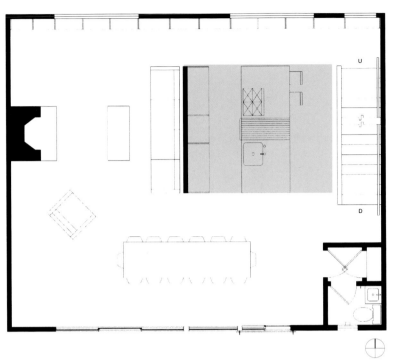

"Functional furniture located within the concrete elements of stair and upstands" INDYK ARCHITECTS

Index of
Architects

Index of Photographers

127

128